BOOK ANALYSIS

Written by Anne Crochet
Translated by Soline de Dorlodot

AF126397

Death Is
My Trade

BY ROBERT MERLE

Bright
≡Summaries.com

ROBERT MERLE

FRENCH WRITER

- **Born in Tebessa (Algeria) in 1908**
- **Died in Grosmouvre in 2004**
- **Notable works:**
  - *Week-end at Zuydcoote* (1949), novel
  - *Death is My Trade* (1952), novel
  - *Fortune de France* (1978-2003), novel

A French writer born in Algeria in 1908, Robert Merle arrived in France in 1918. Having studied English literature, he taught in various high schools and worked as a translator for Gallimard until 1939, when he was enrolled and became a translator for the English troops based in Dunkerque. He was taken prisoner in Germany until 1943, and upon his return to France, he wrote his first novel, *Death is My Trade* (1952), a testimony of Dunkerque's fiasco.

Although Robert Merle's work is as rich as it is diversified (news stories, plays, essays, thriller novels, etc.), the author is most widely known for his historical novels: between 1978 and 2003, he published the thirteen volumes of *Fortune de France*, a historical fresco based on the religious wars, for which he received the Jean Giono award in 2003. He died in 2004.

DEATH IS MY TRADE

INSIDE THE HEAD OF AN SS-OFFICER

- **Genre:** novel
- **Reference edition:** Merle, R. (1952) *La mort est mon métier*. Paris: Gallimard.[1]
- **First edition:** 1952
- **Themes:** Second World War, Nazism, concentration camp, duty Nuremberg trials

Death is My Trade, a historical novel published in 1952, belongs is an example of concentration camp literature, as it explains how the Nazi regime was able to set up the death camps of Auschwitz and Birkenau. The first part of the story is the novelized biography of Rudolf Höss (1900-1947), head of the Auschwitz camp in the 1940s. Based on the notes left by the American psychologist G.M. Gilbert, who interrogated Höss in prison, Robert Merle created a character called Rudolf Lang and imagined what his life would have been like. The second part of the novel is dedicated to the logistics of the conception and the construction of the death camps; to do this, Robert Merle relied on accounts from the Nuremberg trials (1945-1946).

---

1. All quotes are translated by BrightSummaries.com.

SUMMARY

THE LIFE OF A KILLER

In 1913, Rudolf Lang is a 14-year-old German teenager brought up with Christian values. His father, feared by the whole family, wants his son to dedicate his life to the Virgin Mary, in reparation of an adulterous sin he himself committed. However, Rudolf wants to become an officer in the army, like his grandfather. His upbringing taught him a sense of duty, respect, and subordination to authority.

One day, he has an argument with a comrade and accidentally breaks his leg. Panicked, he goes to confess to Father Thaler. Once his father hears the news, he punishes him severely, and Rudolf loses his faith, believing that it is Father Thaler who betrayed the confessional secret and turned him in.

In 1914, after his father's death, Rudolf tries twice to be enrolled for the front, but, as he is too young, he is sent home. He is finally enlisted a few years later and works in the military infirmary. There, he meets the Rittermeister Günther, the captain of the dragoons, who takes a liking to him. Under his influence, Rudolf slowly abandons the family traditions linked to the Church and decides to dedicate himself fully to the salvation of Germany. Then, he decides to change his civil status to "believing in God, not belonging to any confession" (p. 166). He manages to be sent to Irak with the dragoon regiment: he has to fight the British and help the Turks to control the Arab opponents. Mission after mission, Rudolf realizes what his duty implies, but he does not try to shirk it. On Günther's death, the dragoons go back to Germany where they hear that their country has surrendered.

Rudolf, demobilized and unemployed, goes home. His mother has died and his sisters are strangers to him. He leaves his family to join Schräder, a former dragoon. Thanks to him, he finds a job in a factory. However, because of Lang's lack of solidarity with the other workers, the two friends are fired. They are then enrolled in the corps of volunteers on the Western border. Soon after their arrival, they join the Eastern corps of volunteers, who were then considered as the rebels of the German Republic. After Schräder's death and the dissolution of the squad, Rudolf is demobilized once gain.

JOINING THE NATIONAL-SOCIALIST PARTY

Settled in M. for a while, Rudolf has found work on a construction site. Exhausted, famished, poor, and convinced that Germany isn't worth anything anymore, he decides to commit suicide. A colleague prevents him from doing so and puts him in touch with the national-socialist party, which works in favor of the country's rehabilitation. Tasked by the party with the murder of an opponent, Rudolf is arrested and sentenced to ten years in prison at Dachau; he only serves five.

When Rudolf comes out of prison, he is sent to Pomerania by the party. He comes into the employment of the Baron von Jeseritz as a groom. The nobleman asks him to restore an old farm in the marsh, and after having found him a wife, Elsie, he sets them up there. Pushed by von Jeseritz, Rudolf joins the *Bund der Artamen*, a party which defends the German race and soil, and becomes its secretary. He meets Himmler, who orders him to spot and train the militiamen who would later become the SS. In 1932, the party comes to power and Rudolf is made an under-officer in the SS.

Soon, he is offered the position of managing the administration of the concentration camp of Dachau. He hesitates, then accepts, as a service to the party and out of a feeling of duty. When the war breaks out, he wants to be sent to the front, but his request is denied: he is more useful as a part of the administration than on the field. Thus, he is made an officer and is chosen to design and build the concentration camps of Auschwitz (for the Jewish population) and Dachau (for the war prisoners). In 1941, a few months before the opening of the camps, Rudolf learns that Himmler has been chosen to carry out "the final solution to the Jewish problem in Europe" (p. 242). The camp of Auschwitz becomes a death camp whose "maximum efficiency [would reach] ten thousand units a day by 1942" (p. 287). With the help of his underofficers, Rudolf solves the different problems linked to the camps' infrastructure (showers, gas chambers, cremation in the furnaces, mass graves, etc.). Lang's plan is accepted and prepared: everything has to be done by 1942.

From 1943 to 1945, he is appointed camp inspector. In 1945, he receives the order to stop the executions and to do everything he can to reduce the death rate in the camps. In April, Rudolf flees Berlin and hides on a farm. When he hears of

Himmler's suicide, he feels betrayed: the man did not live up to his responsibilities. In 1946, he is arrested by Allied soldiers and put in prison while awaiting the Nuremberg trials, in which he is to act as a prosecution witness. He is then put into the hands of the Polish authorities for his own trial. He is sentenced to be hung in Auschwitz, on one of the gallows he built himself.

CHARACTER STUDY

RUDOLF LANG

The main protagonist and narrator of the novel, Rudolf Lang is a young German (he is 14 at the beginning of the novel) from a family of merchants and officers. His father, a true tyrant, gives him a very strict ultra-Catholic upbringing destined to prepare him for his future clerical life. This conditioning will play an important part in the building of his personality (sense of duty and respect for authority). From his childhood, he also harbors a strong distaste for the Jewish population and the French people.

From the beginning of the story, a brief but comprehensive description enlightens the reader: "Rudolf! You are small, you lack style, you don't talk. But you are smart, educated, and everything you do, you do as a good German is supposed to: thoroughly!" (p. 63).

Throughout the novel, Rudolf Lang is described (by himself or by someone else) as a distanced, insensitive person, who is rarely moved by the plights of others. Although this characteristic might be a problem for his affective and amical life (overall, he does not really care about his family, Elsie, or his friends who died fighting), it is also a tremendous advantage in his military career, as it prevents him from suffering from inner conflicts and therefore, disobeying orders. His dehumanized side is strengthened by his need, when he is anxious, to do mechanical and repetitive actions (walking whilst counting his steps or polishing his shoes). Moreover, it is due to his indifference that he has been chosen to implement the final solution: *"Meine besondere Stärke ist die Praxis"* (p. 231) ("My strong point is practice").

Rudolf also appears as a very obedient character, subordinate to authority, anxious to fulfill his duty and to serve his country. Due to these qualities, he is very appreciated by his hierarchical superiors and he has their trust. The director of the prison, who congratulates him for being honest (Rudolf refused to lie, even though it could have spared him many years of prison), tells him of the danger this characteristic entails: "All honest men are dangerous" (p. 185). He is indeed dangerous, as Rudolf Lang, in obeying Hitler's orders, kills 2,500,000 Jews.

"FATHER"

Rudolf's father, always called "Father", is a very pious fabric merchant. To be absolved of a sin of adultery, he has decided to leave the army and to dedicate his life to the Catholic Church. Deeply religious, he forces his relatives, who fear him, to adopt a rigorous lifestyle, made of privations, duty and repression. He dies in 1914 from a bronchial disease.

Even after his death, he continues to exercise a significant influence over Rudolf Lang's life, who respects him as much as he fears him (p. 29). From his strict catholic upbringing, the young man retained his unwavering subordination to authority, as well as a very acute sense of duty: "Because I taught you – Rudolf- to do your duty – as you clean these windows – thoroughly" (p. 16).

Even though he tries to distance himself from his paternal inheritance, as shown by his abandonment of the Catholic traditions and his detachment from the Church, Rudolf remains imbued with the memory of his father:

> "Strangely, it was in Father's example that I found the strength to overcome these deficiencies. Indeed, I told myself that if Father had found the strength to make each day tremendous sacrifices for a God that did not exist, I, who believed in a tangible ideal, had all the more to give myself up entirely to my faith, without a care for my interest, nor, if need be, my life" (p. 217-218).

It will become apparent later in this analysis that Rudolf seems fascinated by figures of authority that remind him of his father.

COLONEL BARON VON JESERITZ

Colonel Baron von Jeseritz, the owner of a stud farm in Pomerania, welcomes Rudolf when he gets out of prison. Described as "tall and thin, his face tanned and wrinkled" (p. 189), he impresses the main protagonist because of his eyes, whose light can be "unbearable" (p. 189); this look reminds him several times of his father. Very imperious, the baron is an enthusiastic proponent of the German cause. It is for this reason that he entrusts the management of a farm on his Pomeranian lands to Rudolf, in order to stem the arrival of Slavs in that region. Von Jeseritz is at the origin of the main protagonist's meeting with Himmler, and organized Rudolf's marriage to Elsie himself.

THE REICHSFÜHRER HEINRICH HIMMLER

Rudolf meets Himmler through the intermediary of the Baron von Jeseritz. At first, he only notices his fat and plump hands, before hearing his voice: "His voice was flat and toneless, but he talked a lot, without hesitation, without pause, absolutely as if he was reading a book" (p. 212). Not much is known about this character, except that he is cunning.

Himmler plays an important role in Rudolf's existence, in that it is he who gives him the task to design and build the death camps. When he commits suicide in 1945, Rudolf feels deeply betrayed and abandoned.

ELSIE

Elsie Brücker is the daughter of Wilhelm, a farmer who works for the Baron von Jeseritz. She has been chosen by the Baron to become Rudolf's wife. Elsie admires Rudolf for the work he accomplished on the farm and agrees to marry him. Throughout their marriage, the young woman shows herself to be understanding and loving, willful, hard-working and able to renounce her personal dreams so that her husband can pursue his military career. However, she often complains to Rudolf about his lack of interest and affection: "Sometimes, when you are sitting at the table and looking at nothing with your cold eyes, I get the impression that I don't really matter" (p. 211). Elsie doesn't know anything about the special operation organized by her husband in the concentration camps. When she hears of it by accident, she is revolted by these massacres and does not understand how he could do such a thing. Therefore, Elsie represents this part of humanity that is lacking in her husband.

THE OBERSTURMFÜHRER SETZLER

Setzler, a lieutenant in the S.S. army, is one of Rudolf's right hand men: he helps him to find solutions to the problems encountered during the building of the death camps. Thin and bald, he is said to be quick to blush when he is moved, that he is rather sensitive and that he has the soul of an artist (supposed to explain this sensitivity). After some time, Setzler confesses to Rudolf that he cannot bear the smell of burning flesh or the cries of the prisoners anymore; he asks to be sent to the front. However, Rudolf refuses to give him a recommendation letter to allow this. Out of despair, Setzler commits suicide. Like Elsie, he represents the humanity that the main character is lacking.

ANALYSIS

THE OMNIPRESENCE OF THE FATHER, A FIGURE OF AUTHORITY

As seen above, Rudolf's relation to his father was rather complex, lying somewhere between obedience, fear and respect. "Father", who was the most determining figure of the protagonist's childhood, is embodied in different ways by other authoritative characters of the novel, who will condition him and guide the existence of the future commander of Auschwitz.

Rittmeister Günther

Captain of the dragoons, Günther pushed Rudolf, then aged 16, to enlist in his regiment. He shares the same convictions as "Father" concerning the duties of a German: to do things thoroughly. "'Everything you do, you do like a good German should: thoroughly!' he says this with the same intonation as Father and, I think, nearly with the same voice" (p. 64-65), as Rudolf explains. The faith that Father had in his Church, Günther has in the army and in Germany: "*Meine Kirche heisst Deutschland*" ("My Church is called Germany", p. 69). Although these two faiths might seem contradictory, they both underline the necessity for total subordination to a superior (religion and the German government).

Colonel Baron von Jeseritz

The Baron's authority and pangermanism, as well as his determination, are reminiscent of Rudolf's father: like the father figure, he decides Rudolf's future by ordering him to marry Elsie and to live on one of his farms. The main protagonist fears von Jeseritz and his look: "He looked at me: These were [sic] the eyes of father. A lump formed in my throat, I could not talk" (p. 205).

Heinrich Himmler

Himmler seems less authoritative than the previous characters. His intelligence attracts Rudolf, as well as the trust he puts in him (Himmler puts him in charge of several concentration camps). Therefore, Himmler is the character who is the farthest away from the father figure, but it is he who generates a feeling of filial piety the most. Indeed, when Himmler commits suicide, Rudolf feels betrayed and abandoned: "Don't you understand? He backed out! ... He whom I respected like a father" (p. 357).

Thus, the father, who dies at the beginning of the novel, stays at the forefront throughout the whole story: Rudolf is fascinated by the characters that have the same psychological profile. Himmler is the only exception to this rule, as he embodies the true father rather than an authoritative figure to be feared.

A DEHUMANIZED NOVEL

Death is My Trade discusses the topic of the death camps in a very cold and clinical way. This approach, chosen by Robert Merle, is the consequence of the choice of Rudolf Lang as the narrator. The insensitive nature of the character indeed has an impact on the narration: few words belonging to the lexical field of feelings are used, the textual space dedicated to supposedly strong moments of his existence (the death of his father, his first sexual experience, his wedding) is very limited, and the succession of facts is comparatively highlighted. For example, at the death of his father: "On 15th May 1914, Father died, the routine of the household remained unchanged, I continued to attend Mass every morning, Mother took over the store and our material situation improved" (p. 52). In this extract, the narrator insists on the pragmatic consequences of the events rather than on the emotions generated, despite the father being an important figure in Rudolf's life.

Present in the story from different perspectives, this global dehumanization resulted in the objectification of the novel's characters, especially the Jewish population and prisoners. As Rudolf considers them objects, the narration must mirror this thought: "You see, I thought of the Jews in terms of units, never in terms of human beings. I focused solely on the technical aspect of my task" (p. 363); "The capacity of Treblinka was of 300 units per 24 hours, that of Auschwitz, according to the program, was to be of 3000 units" (p. 267).

THE IMPORTANCE OF DUTY

The notion of duty is very present in the novel, especially in the military characters' minds. As Rudolf's father had heavily insisted on the obligation to fulfill one's duty towards the Church, the young man very naturally transposes this feeling when he joins the S.S. army, whose motto is "My honor [...] is loyalty" (p. 224). Loyalty towards one's hierarchical superior implies total obedience: "Our duty, our only duty, was obeying. And thanks to this absolute obedience, [...] we were sure to never make mistakes" (p. 224). Following this principle, Rudolf blindly obeys the extermination order given by Himmler: if Himmler is asking him to execute the Jewish population, it must be done. The struggles of conscience and the responsibility of the subordinate are therefore inexistent, as in theory, it is the one who gives the orders who shoulders the responsibility of the actions perpetrated by his lieutenants. The one who performs the action has nothing to worry about, aside from accomplishing his task well.

The need to fulfill his duty towards Germany governs Rudolf's existence, as seen in many abstracts dedicated to this topic (p. 127; p. 217-218; p. 340-345; p. 362-364): "I do not need excuses. I obeyed" (p. 362); "I can't be concerned about what I think. My duty is to obey" (p. 363). The personal wishes of Rudolf and his wife are swept away by the duty to their fatherland. Rudolf will never question the notion of duty, not even during his process in Warsaw: although he regrets having killed many Jews, This is only because he obeyed someone who did not deserve it (Himmler), rather than out of compassion for his victims. It is this aspect of Rudolf's personality which seems to have made the deepest impression on Robert Merle: "Everything Rudolf did, he did not out of meanness, but in the name of a categorical imperative, out of loyalty to the leader, out of subordination to order, out of respect for the State. In brief, a *man of duty*: and it is exactly in this that he is monstrous" (Preface).

FURTHER REFLECTION

SOME QUESTIONS TO THINK ABOUT...

- In the 1960s, Stanley Milgram led an experiment aiming to evaluate the degree of subordination of a random citizen to the representative of a legitimate authority. Explain how Milgram's experiment compares to *Death is My Trade*.
- "I do not need excuses. I obeyed" (p. 362). Explain how, according to Rudolf, this sentence justifies his actions.
- Which characters in the novel embody the authority of the father figure? Justify your answer by using examples from the text.
- *Les Bienveillantes* (2006) by Jonathan Littell tells the story of Maximilien Aue, an S.S. officer who took part in the Nazi massacres. Compare the way the two protagonists (Maximilien Aue and Rudolf Lang) act and think.
- In the preface, written in 1972, Robert Merle describes Rudolf Lang as follow : "Under the Nazi regime, there were hundreds, thousands of Rudolf Langs, moral within immorality, conscientious but without conscience, small employees acceding to high positions because of their seriousness and their 'merits'" (Preface). Comment on this quote.
- How are the theses of Hannah Arendt about the banality of evil ((ARENDT H., *Eichmann à Jérusalem. Rapport sur la banalité du mal*, Paris, Gallimard, 1966) illustrated in *Death is My Trade*? Justify your answer by using examples from the text.
- When he hears of Himmler's suicide, Rudolf feels

betrayed: "I couldn't talk anymore. Pain and shame were suffocating me. Neither exile nor the defeat had impressed me more" (p. 357). In your opinion, why does Rudolf react like that?

We want to hear from you!
Leave a comment on your online library
and share your favourite books on social media!

FURTHER READING

REFERENCE EDITION

- Merle, R. (1952) *La mort est mon métier*. Paris: Gallimard, 1952.

REFERENCE STUDIES

- Arendt, H. (1966) *Eichmann à Jérusalem. Rapport sur la banalité du mal*. Paris: Gallimard.
- Gilbert, G. (1947) *Le Journal de Nuremberg*. Paris: Flammarion.
- Höss, R. (2005) *Le commandant d'Auschwitz parle*. Paris: La Découverte.
- Littell, J. (2006) *Les Bienveillantes*. Paris: Gallimard.
- Milgram, S. (1974) *Obedience to Authority. An Experimental View*. New York: Harper Perennial Classic.

©BrightSummaries.com, 2016. All rights reserved.

www.brightsummaries.com

Ebook EAN: 9782806270474

Paperback EAN: 9782806274489

Legal Deposit: D/2015/12603/628

Cover: © Primento

Digital conception by Primento, the digital partner of publishers.